Original title:

Sands of Solace

Copyright © 2025 Creative Arts Management OÜ
All rights reserved.

Author: Nash Everly
ISBN HARDBACK: 978-1-80581-693-5
ISBN PAPERBACK: 978-1-80581-220-3
ISBN EBOOK: 978-1-80581-693-5

Forgotten Stories of the Earth

In the garden, weeds wear crowns,
While carrots dance in silly gowns.
The sun winks with a golden glow,
As worms recite their wit and woe.

Old rocks gossip, tales unfold,
Of socks once lost, and sandwiches bold.
The breeze giggles, tickles the trees,
As grasshoppers hum jazzy melodies.

The ants march in a grand parade,
With tiny flags, they're never afraid.
They tell of crumbs from a picnic spread,
As squirrels chuckle, "You missed the bread!"

At dusk, the shadows play a trick,
They dance like fools, each move a kick.
Forgotten stories swirl and twirl,
In the whispers of a giggling world.

Hearth of the Heart

In the kitchen, pots tap dance loud,
While muffins rise to make them proud.
The spoons debate who's number one,
As cookies giggle, "We'll have our fun!"

The kettle sings a bubbling tune,
While sugar lumps play hide and swoon.
The oven grins with a warm embrace,
Turning up the heat in a friendly race.

Tongs and spatulas form a band,
With a whisk as the drum, it's all quite grand.
Spices swirl with a joyful cheer,
As the flour says, "I'm here for a career!"

When all is done, a feast appears,
The table laughs, and everyone cheers.
In the hearth where love is stirred,
An appetizing joke is always heard.

A Quiet Haven

In a corner where laughter pretends,
A cat steals a sock while the dog just bends.
Tea sets are gossiping soft in the sun,
While a squirrel in a tie thinks he's just had fun.

A frog in a hat jumps and cheekily croaks,
The parakeets squabble, they're chirpy little blokes.
Whispers of mischief float on the breeze,
As the garden grows jests among the tall trees.

Solitary Voyage

I set sail on a boat made of cheese,
With a crew of dandelions swaying at ease.
The sea was a pudding, the sun was a spoon,
And we danced on the waves under a jellybean moon.

The captain, a turtle, wore spectacles bright,
As we navigated seas of pure daydream delight.
Beneath us, the fish wore top hats and capes,
While we sang silly songs about cupcakes and grapes.

Fleeting Moments in the Heat

Under the sun, we flopped like old fish,
Ice cream dribbled down every young wish.
The grass tickled toes as we sprawled in a heap,
While ants served us snacks as we fell fast asleep.

The lemonade turned to a hot, mushy mess,
Why did I wear this old summer dress?
In the chaos of fun, nothing seemed right,
But the laughter was endless, shining so bright.

The Stillness of Forgotten Paths

Down old routes where the grass likes to play,
A gopher in shades thinks he's king for the day.
With a squirrel as a sidekick, they take on the night,
In a quest for the best nut - it's quite the sight!

The paths whisper secrets of what came before,
Like a cat who once dreamt he could open doors.
With each little stumble, we trip and we fall,
In the laughter and giggles, we're kings of it all.

Hushed Wishes Beneath the Sky

The stars hold secrets, they whisper and giggle,
As I tripped on a rock and did a little wiggle.
A wish floats by on a chubby old cloud,
I hope it's not shy, and I wish it out loud.

Dreams tumble like tumbleweeds, round and around,
I chase them with laughter, they seem to have found.
A moonbeam steals cookies from warm, sleepy pies,
While crickets in bow ties propose grand goodbyes.

Tides of Time

The waves are all beckoning, I dive with a flip,
But surfboards are slippery, oh dear, what a slip!
They chuckle and roll, the ocean can tease,
While I'm dodging seagulls, just trying to freeze.

Time trickles like sand through an hourglass fast,
But it's stuck in my shoe as I race and I blast.
With each goofy dance on the shore and the foam,
I question if mermaids would welcome me home.

Elysian Echoes

In a garden of giggles, I sit on a flower,
It sneezes and rustles, what a sneeze of power!
The blooms are all chuckling, they spread silly cheer,
I wonder if gnomes ever drink kegs full of beer.

Echoes of laughter bounce off the tall trees,
If trees could speak, what would they say, please?
I join in their laughter, it wiggles my brain,
In a world full of joy, who'd complain or feel pain?

Caress of the Whispering Wind

The breeze gives me hugs, as it twirls through my hair,
It's whispering secrets, but I just can't seem to care.
I dance with the leaves, they giggle and sway,
While I try to convince them to join my ballet.

In the caress of the wind, I feel like a fool,
A squirrel joins the show, diving into the pool.
With twirls and hops, we form a wild band,
Making mischief with each grain of dust from the land.

Time's Gentle Caress

Oh, look at that clock, it's moving slow,
Like a turtle in slippers, don't you know?
Time's tick-tocking, but I'm cozy in hair,
I'll just sip my tea and pretend I don't care.

Sunrise to sunset, what a sight to behold,
Yet I'm still in my PJs, feeling quite bold.
The day drags on like a long-winded tale,
But laughter and snacks will make sure I prevail.

Footprints of Reflection

In the sand, my thoughts scatter around,
Like kids at a fair, all lost and unbound.
I tripped on a memory, fell flat on my face,
But got up with a grin, it's all just a race!

Each footprint I leave tells a joke of its own,
One foot's a dancer, the other's a drone.
I slip on the laughter, I trip over bliss,
In the mess of the moments, I find my purest kiss.

A Quiet Stroll Through Time

A stroll through the years, so quiet and slick,
Like a cat on a hot tin roof, quick, quick, quick!
I greet every moment with a chuckle and grin,
For time's just a prankster, let the games begin!

The past is a riddle, wrapped tight in a song,
But I dance through the echoes, where I belong.
With each little giggle, I gather my cheer,
In the puzzle of laughter, I've nothing to fear.

The Desert's Lullaby

The desert sings softly, its notes full of jest,
Where cacti are dancers, they're simply the best.
A lizard rolls by, wearing shades and a smile,
He struts like a model, it's all in his style.

The sun takes a bow, showing off its bright glow,
Where mirages give winks in a dizzying show.
I laugh with the winds, they tickle my name,
In this wild, sandy circus, it's all just a game.

Mirage of Rest

In the desert, I found a chair,
It wobbled, but I didn't care.
The sun laughed, I thought I'd snooze,
But my drink vanished, just like my shoes.

Cacti giggled as I sipped sand,
A mirage teased, but oh, so bland.
I chased a llama for my shade,
Turns out it was a cactus trade.

A breeze blew whispers, funny and light,
My thoughts drifted like a kite in flight.
I lay back, stars above, so bright,
Dreaming of snacks, but it's still daylight!

I woke to find a squirrel nearby,
With a tiny sombrero, oh my, oh my!
We shared a laugh, the best of friends,
In this strange land where humor never ends.

Beneath the Endless Sky

Beneath the sky, a blanket wide,
I spread my arms, and I just sighed.
The clouds above were all in jest,
A shower of laughs, a humorous fest.

A tumbleweed rolled by with glee,
Tickled my toes, what a sight to see!
I joined the dance, my hat took flight,
Chasing it down, what a glorious plight!

The sun smiled down, a cheeky grin,
I tried to outsmart it, but where to begin?
With sunscreen slathered, I made a stand,
But soon found a squirrel had stolen my brand.

Donkeys played poker by a dusty trail,
Counting their chips, they began to wail.
I laughed so hard, I nearly cried,
Beneath the sky, where joy can't hide.

Refuge in the Arid Land

In an arid land, I found a cave,
But instead of peace, it smelled quite brave.
A lizard winked, like a wise old sage,
"Come for refuge, at your age!"

Turned out the cave was a lizard's den,
With snacks of crickets, I'd dive right in.
But every bite would lead to a laugh,
As I munched and crunched, losing my path.

A tumble here, a stumble there,
Laughter echoed, splitting the air.
I chased my hat—oh, what a sight,
A weary lizard found great delight.

At sunset's glow, the shadows danced,
In this arid land, I took a chance.
Finding refuge, with laughter entwined,
A joyful heart is the best you can find.

Oasis in the Heart

An oasis bloomed inside my chest,
A curious place, where jesters rest.
Sipping sunshine from a grand old tree,
I looked around, what a sight to see!

Big birds played cards, gossip in the air,
Tales of grand feasts, beyond compare.
I chuckled aloud, feeling so light,
In this playful haven, nothing felt tight.

A monkey swung down, "What's your plan?"
I said, "Just laughing, and maybe a tan!"
He threw me coconuts, one after another,
In this quirky spot, we became like brothers.

The breeze whispered secrets, funny and bright,
An oasis of laughter felt just right.
In the heart of joy, I made my mark,
Finding fun in the wild—a delightful spark.

Fragments of Forgotten Echoes

In a land where marbles bounce,
The whispers of past puns still pounce.
Laughter echoes off the walls,
Like tiny critters doing the crawls.

Surfers ride on jelly waves,
While daydreaming about lost graves.
A taco talks, a pie tells jokes,
As fish play chess, surrounded by folks.

Naps are timely with no regrets,
While seagulls boast of fishing bets.
A cat brought snacks on a float, you see,
Spreading cheer from sea to brie.

So let the anchors weigh your heart,
While comedy plays its silly part.
In haha phantoms we shall bask,
As giggles drown all serious tasks.

Serenity in the Silence

There's a lawn chair with a flair,
Where a turtle's bustling without a care.
A rubber duck just made a sale,
It's now the captain of a wooden whale.

Clouds play peek-a-boo with the sun,
And broccoli claims it's the biggest fun.
Moonlight whispers to the night,
While squirrels dance, all feeling right.

The wind sings songs with a funny twist,
Inviting all the stars to join the list.
With each breeze, a chuckle flies,
As sleepy walls tell secret lies.

So sit and sip your fizzy drink,
Let pigeons perch and dogs just wink.
In silence, let the nonsense flow,
As laughter's seeds begin to grow.

Grain of Comfort

Once a kernel dreamed to fly,
But got stuck in a popper pie.
With every jump, it rolled away,
To find a world full of parfaits.

Pancakes pogo on the stove,
As jam and cream find ways to rove.
A flick of syrup, a dance so sweet,
As waffles join in, tapping their feet.

So gather round the breakfast tale,
Where biscuits sail and muffins grail.
With smiles smeared in berry bliss,
Each bite is worth a crunchy kiss.

And when the syrup starts to spill,
We'll laugh and stack it up until,
The grain of joy warms every heart,
In breakfast brawls, we play our part.

Harmony in the Heat

A sunburned crab composed a tune,
While juggling seashells beneath the moon.
The waves applauded with their roar,
As a starfish tried to tap dance on the shore.

Ice cream cones wore tiny hats,
While penguins blasted with karaoke chats.
Coconuts began to sing,
As dolphins pranced in a rubber ring.

When the sky blushed with cotton candy,
And summer danced just a bit too dandy,
Lemons formed a marching band,
While pickles had their own hot stand.

So let's embrace this sunny show,
Where giggles flow and breezes blow.
In harmony, let's barbecue
With laughter sizzled just for you!

Breath of the Quiet Breeze

Whispers dance through sunny trees,
Where grasshoppers play in the gentle tease.
A duck wearing sunglasses strolls by,
With no sense of rush, just a leisurely sigh.

Clouds shaped like marshmallows drift high,
As squirrels debate on who's got the best pie.
Yet the breeze chuckles, carrying the sound,
Of laughter that rolls across the ground.

A cat in a hammock, swaying away,
Dreams of fish, oh, what a fine day!
The chill of the night makes them all stammer,
As stars fall down like a cosmic glamor.

Timeless Shadows of Solace

The wall clock's melting, what a sight!
Time's tick turned into a silly flight.
A turtle rushes by, wearing a cap,
And whispers sweet nothings with a little clap.

Shadows dance, they trip and fall,
One gets up and starts to sprawl.
A wise old owl just shakes its head,
'Time is a joke, better stay in bed!'

The merry sun spills laughter anew,
As morning glories yawn to break through.
Yet the clock just grins, trying to tease,
In a world where nothing is quite as it seems.

Glistening Grain of Comfort

In fields where grains whisper to the breeze,
Each stalk tells tales of sunny teas.
Bunnies hop in hats, so deranged,
Planning a party, perfectly arranged.

The wheat wears a smile as tall as a tree,
While ants march in line, a parade with glee.
A scarecrow takes selfies with a grin,
Dancing to tunes of old-fashioned jazz within.

Butterflies laugh, flaunting their wings,
While corn cobs dream of purple bling.
The golden fields sway in a silly trance,
As crickets set off in a lively dance.

Solitary Mirage Beneath the Stars

A lone cactus dons a stylish hat,
Under stars that wink, 'What's up with that?'
A lizard sings to a moon so bright,
While owls roll their eyes, ready for flight.

The night air's crackling with jokes so grand,
As tumbleweeds twirl like they're in a band.
A cowboy clown prances with flair,
Whispering secrets to the cool night air.

Beneath the vastness, a giggle is heard,
As galaxies chuckle at every word.
The sand whispers tales of dreamers afar,
In this mirage where wishes now spar.

Traces of Tranquil Wanderings

Lost my shoes on a sunny spree,
Who knew the beach would steal from me?
A crab waved hello, a seagull said bye,
Now I'm barefoot, with sand in my eye.

Footprints lead to snacks, a treasure trove,
Ice cream drips down, making a mess, oh cove!
The sun laughs at my floppy hat's flight,
As I chase after it, what a silly sight!

Waves roll in with a cheerful tease,
I do the splash dance with utmost ease.
Yet the tide has plans, it pulls my feet,
I stumble back, never tasted defeat!

I'll wander the shores, my heart full of glee,
Chasing down laughter, just like the sea.
Beach bum adventures, all wrapped in delight,
Under the sun, everything feels just right.

Veil of Twilight Reverie

Twilight settles, the sky's a peach,
But look out, here comes a funny beach screech.
A tired gull plus a crab on patrol,
Makes for a sight, oh what a goal!

Sunset drapes like a colorful shawl,
I tripped on my towel, oh what a fall!
Sandcastles stand tall, I gave them a grin,
Until a wave sneezes, "Let the fun begin!"

Laughing shadows dance in the glow,
Where flip-flops flop and giggles flow.
A jellyfish jigs, oh what a hit,
Next to my cooler, sticky and lit!

As day turns to night, the starlight beams,
Drifting in visions, I'm lost in dreams.
Life's just a whirl, a joyful spree,
With sandy toes, I am completely free.

Beneath the Weight of Time

Time tick-tocks with a sandy laugh,
I paused to pose for a grumpy calf.
Waves go rushing, as seagulls squawk,
Like life is a dance, a funny walk.

An hourglass spills with a playful clink,
I catch my breath and spill my drink.
Time's up! says the tide, with a friendly nudge,
But here on the shore, I refuse to judge.

A starfish grins with a bit of flair,
While turtles swim, as if in a dare.
The clock's gone mad, no reason to hurry,
Just me and the beach, it's all quite blurry.

With grains of laughter still stuck in my hair,
I treasure these moments, a sea of rare.
Under the weight of time, it's a whimsical race,
On this sandy path, I've found my place.

Stillness in the Affectionate Sands

In the stillness where giggles reside,
The beach rolls in like an eager tide.
Sunshine kisses my freckled nose,
While a sandman chuckles in humorous prose.

Shells whisper secrets, a playful tease,
Caught in the current of a gentle breeze.
The sun's a joker, playing hide and seek,
With each little wave, laughter will peak.

But oh, watch out for that seagull's gift,
A swoop and a dive, and there goes my lift!
Ice cream bloopers, oh the sticky thrill,
As I tack on moments, they fit like a quill.

In this tranquil place where the gulls spin and sway,
I find my joy in the light of the day.
Life's a comedy, with ups and downs,
In affectionate sands, we're all wearing crowns!

Deserted Heartstrings

In the desert, my heart does roam,
Looking for laughs, not a place called home.
Cacti wave like friends in cheer,
While I stumble upon my own rear.

Lizards dance in shades of brown,
Wearing tiny sunglasses, never a frown.
They laugh at me, lost on my way,
Every step feels like a comedic play.

The sun beats down, I take a break,
A mirage of ice cream makes my heart ache.
But as I reach for that delicious cone,
It's just a rock trying to be shown.

Yet through the sand, I find my groove,
Jokes on repeat, a dance to prove.
In this barren land, laughter springs,
A heart once heavy, now freely sings.

Tranquil Reverie

In a world where silence reigns supreme,
I chase a dream, or so it would seem.
A tumbleweed rolls by, in no hurry,
Mocking my thoughts, oh what a flurry!

The sun sets slowly, a golden hue,
I wave at the moon, it waves back too.
Stars giggle softly, twinkling bright,
Whispering secrets in the cool night light.

A tumble through twilight, a laugh-filled spree,
My mind takes a stroll; it's so carefree.
With every breath, I find a joke,
In this tranquil place, I am bespoke.

What if I tripped over a cactus bloom?
I'd say, "How rude!" before meeting my doom.
But it's all in good fun, in gentle repose,
In my joyful slumber, chuckles impose.

Silent Footprints

Footprints in the dust, quite the sight,
They tell tales of mishaps under the light.
Each step I take, a mini disaster,
My balance fails, but I'm still a master.

The quiet whispers secrets untold,
Like how my hat flew off, oh so bold.
Chasing it down, a sight to behold,
A comic relief against the world's cold.

The echoes of laughter dance on the breeze,
While the sun plays tag with the desert trees.
Yet I march on, a hero unmasked,
Collecting the giggles, a daunting task.

Tripping on stones, I take my bow,
My silent footprints, my own little vow.
In a land of stillness, comedy thrives,
Finding joy in the dust, where humor survives.

Harmony Beneath the Stars

Under a blanket of shimmering night,
I strum my guitar, but what a fright!
The strings are off, my notes askew,
Even the coyotes join in the boo-hoo.

Stars above twinkle, full of glee,
While I attempt a tune, maybe just flee.
My serenade turns into a jest,
Even the crickets seem unimpressed!

But what's a heart without a good laugh?
I stomp my feet, I'll call it my craft.
The desert joins in, with sand in my shoe,
As I dance like no one's watching, it's true!

In this cosmic nightlife, I find my place,
With humor and joy, I embrace the space.
Beneath the stars, mischief and fun,
In the great comedy show, we're all one.

Nightfall's Embrace

As twilight comes in a big gray hat,
The moon does a tango with a nearby cat.
Stars giggle softly, oh what a sight,
While owls in pajamas take flight in the night.

The crickets play music, a jolly old tune,
While mice wear top hats and waltz by the moon.
Fireflies dance like they're lost in a trance,
Filling the dark with their flickering prance.

Bats offer drinks from a tiny bar stool,
And all of the shadows play hopscotch, how cool!
A jester named Nightfall brings joy with a wink,
Inviting us all for a moment to think.

So laugh at the darkness, don't worry or fret,
The silliness lingers, you won't soon forget.
In the embrace of night full of whimsy and cheer,
We find our own solace, no worry, no fear.

Veil of Dust

In a world where dust bunnies mischievously play,
One's wearing a crown, what a sight to display!
While chairs take a nap and the tables do sneak,
The vacuum's out dancing; it must be a week.

Shadows are gossiping, sharing their tales,
Of curious creatures who chew on their nails.
The dust motes are jumping, they sparkle and swirl,
As the clock on the wall performs its own twirl.

A wizard of cleaning is making his rounds,
Tap dancing on floors with the most cheerful sounds.
And mugs in the cupboards, they clink with delight,
As they toast to the mess that makes everything bright.

So cheer for the dust, let it settle with style,
For what's life without laughter, in every while?
Raise your dusty arms and dance with the mess,
In the veil of the fun, find your own happiness.

A Retreat Within

I found a small nook where the pillows do laugh,
They tell silly stories, oh what a gaffe!
With tea cups that giggle and blankets that hum,
This cozy retreat beckons all who feel glum.

The door creaks open with a squeaky old song,
While cushions sit quiet, all the day long.
I tripped on a sock that was plotting a flight,
And landed in laughter as if it were right.

A cat with a hat thinks he's king of this throne,
While books whisper secrets, their pages well-known.
The clock likes to tick-tock, but it does so with glee,
Count down all the moments of joy, clearly free.

So here in my haven where the giggles arise,
I'll stay for a while, beneath soft, fluffy skies.
With laughter as currency, peace as my kin,
In this fluffy retreat, let the fun times begin.

Echoes of Elation

There's a sound in the air that tickles the toes,
Like whispers from bubbles that giggle and pose.
A chorus of chortles floats high in the breeze,
In the land where the jesters have laughter with ease.

Marshmallows skip while the cookies do twirl,
And sprinkles breakdance in a sugary whirl.
A cake takes a bow, with fondant so grand,
As the jellybeans jive to the beat of the band.

Lollipops join in with a top hat and cane,
While fruit gummis wiggle, oh what a domain!
Tickled by sunshine, they sparkle and shine,
These sweet little echoes are yours and are mine.

So let's all join in on this merry-go-round,
With laughter as fuel, we won't tire or drown.
For in every giggle, we may find our fate,
In echoes of joy, let's celebrate!

The Solace of Endless Horizons

A beach ball bounces, what a sight,
Chasing the seagulls, takes to flight.
Flip-flops flapping, oh what a race,
With ocean spray, it's a splashy embrace.

Sandcastles crumble like dreams gone wild,
Waves crash in, but we laugh like a child.
Laughter echoes as seagulls dive,
Collecting treasures, we feel so alive.

Kites soar high, doing flips and spins,
While sunscreen's smeared, oh where to begin?
With a wink and a chuckle, we twirl in the breeze,
As the sun dips low, we're buzzing like bees.

So let's dance on the shore, carefree and spry,
With salty spritzes, we'll reach for the sky.
Life's a sandy party, come join the fun,
In this endless horizon, we've all just begun.

Nature's Breathing Canvas

Painted leaves whisper, nature's delight,
The brush of the wind, an artist's insight.
Brush strokes of green and sunlit gold,
Every hue tells a story, yet to unfold.

Bumblebees buzzing, wearing a hat,
Dancing on blooms, now where's the cat?
With frolicsome frogs and a chuckling breeze,
Nature's a comic, bringing us to our knees.

Clouds in the sky, like cotton candy spun,
Chasing rainbows, oh let's run, run, run!
Petals fall softly as giggles abound,
Each moment's a treasure waiting to be found.

So let's sketch the world with laughter and cheer,
Nature's a muse; let's hold her dear.
With breezy antics and colors so bright,
We'll paint our adventure from morning to night.

Whispers of Dunes

In the desert's heart, a tumbleweed rolls,
A wacky dance, where the cacti have souls.
Footprints that vanish, a silly charade,
With each gust of wind, our worries cascade.

Silly lizards frolic, on tiny adventures,
With sand in their toes, they seek new ventures.
As mirages tease, with drinks that won't stay,
We giggle at shadows that lead us astray.

A dandy picnic, with ants in a line,
Trying to steal our snacks, oh so divine!
The sunflowers wave, with a grin on their face,
In this barren beauty, we find our place.

So here's to the dunes, where laughter flows free,
With whispers of joy from the cactus to sea.
Let's ride on the tides of whimsy and grace,
In this land of mirth, we've found our space.

Shifting Echoes

Echoes of chuckles in a windy locale,
As tumbleweeds tumble, we all start to howl.
The footprints we leave, like a comical cue,
In this shifting landscape, we'll make our debut.

A dance with the coyotes, what a spectacle!
They howl their lyrics, it's quite the pectoral.
With desert delight in every shy glance,
We join the parade, in a joyful prance.

The stars overhead twinkle like giggles,
While shadows all sway, do the silly wiggles.
In this land of mirth, where fun fills the air,
With echoes of laughter, who needs to compare?

So let's paint our journey with lighthearted cheer,
In this wide-open place, may all magic appear.
With each playful step, let's cherish the day,
In the shifting echoes, let's laugh all the way.

Oasis of Lost Moments

In a desert of socks, I find my shoe,
My cat thinks it's dinner, but it just won't do.
The sunbeam's a spotlight on my messy pile,
I dance with my shadows, embracing the mile.

A mirage of dinner, an illusion of cake,
The fridge has its secrets, it's surely a fake.
A squirrel steals my sandwich, what a bold thief,
Yet I laugh, as I stumble, my heart believes.

I chased a lost button across the great floor,
It rolled under the couch, oh what a chore!
My dog gives a snort, then jumps on my lap,
Together we ponder, is this life a wrap?

In this silly little place, where moments collide,
I smile at the chaos, there's joy in the ride.
So here's to the laughter, each flub and each fall,
For in this crazy life, we're alive after all!

Murmurs Beneath the Surface

In the depths of my pockets, old gum finds a home,
With crumbs of my past, it feels like a poem.
A sea of lost marbles, I search in despair,
But finding a button? Now that's quite rare!

Each wave's a new giggle, oh how it can tease,
My phone plays hide and seek, like it's trying to flee.
The fish stare in wonder, what's this human mess?
I wave at the dolphins, they seem to impress.

Bubbles of laughter, they pop in the air,
As I trip over flip-flops, without a care.
The driftwood's a treasure, a chair in disguise,
I lounge, sip my drink, while the seagull just flies.

So here's to the water, where giggles take flight,
A splash of absurdity makes everything bright.
Tomorrow's another, with magic and fun,
We'll ride the strange waves, until day is done!

The Calm After the Storm

After wild winds howl, the house starts to creak,
I survey the treasures, where did my shoe sneak?
The umbrella is dancing, a sad little sight,
While the chaos takes pause, everything's quite bright.

The plants wave hello, a quirky green crew,
They've weathered the tempest, mustache-like dew.
The cat's on the windowsill, judging the sky,
"Such drama," she ponders, as clouds float by.

With jellybean rainbows now strung in the air,
I tiptoe through puddles, my socks want to flare.
A duck makes a quack, his dance is a tease,
I mirror his moves under drizzling trees.

So here's to the calm, where giggles resound,
As shadows relax, and peace can be found.
Let's toast to the mayhem, the wacky delight,
For after the storm, it all feels just right!

Reflections on a Sea of Stillness

The stillness is tricky, like jelly on toast,
It jiggles and wobbles, yet gives me a boast.
The mirror reflects all my silly mishaps,
With hairdos all wacky, and missing my snaps.

I ponder a puddle, it whispers my name,
"Jump in for a splash, it's a hilarious game!"
The frogs serenade, as I giggle and sway,
While the clouds play tag in a whimsical way.

Each ripple's a chuckle, a peaceful delight,
I sink in the stillness, it feels just right.
So, I'll splash with abandon, in joy I'll submerge,
For life's a grand circus, let's joyfully verge!

With moments like shadows, we'll dance 'til we tire,
Our laughter the music, our hearts set afire.
In a world of still waters, frivolous fun,
We'll float on the laughter, our journey's begun!

Dreaming in the Desert

A cactus wears a silly hat,
With shades and sandals, how about that?
Lizards dance in the midday glow,
While camels prance, putting on a show.

The sun is hot, but spirits are high,
As tumbleweeds roll and say hi,
Under a sky that's oh so blue,
I lost my shoe, now what to do?

Sandcastles rise, a king's grand quest,
But the royal moat is a cactus fest,
With every grain, a tale unfolds,
Of sunburned noses and treasures bold.

In this dry land, laughter we find,
With jokes that tickle the sandy mind,
So let's toast with cactus juice,
In silly shorts, we cut loose.

Enigma of the Arid

Oh what a riddle, this desert wide,
Where socks can vanish, no place to hide,
The mirage giggles, "Catch me if you can!"
But all drivers end up as a sand-blown fan.

Talking lizards wear glasses, it's true,
While hissing winds sing a lullaby too,
As I run from shadows of rocks that sway,
Is that a figment or just a play?

The sand dunes tease with a playful pout,
Making me wonder what it's all about,
Will I find treasure or a lost shoe?
Or just more heat and a sunburned hue?

Jokes float like dust, a whimsical tune,
Hoping to meet the wise old raccoon,
In this dry land, we joke and we cheer,
With cacti high-fives, foiling all fear.

Peace Beneath the Open Sky

Kites made of feathers, flying up high,
While I trip over tumbleweed—oh my!
The breeze carries whispers, a jest in the air,
As I lounge on my blanket with not a care.

Birds wear tuxedos, a formal delight,
And squirrels throw parties, a comical sight,
Under the stars, they dance with such grace,
While I'm just trying to keep up the pace.

A moonlit giggle fills the starry dome,
Chasing laughter like it's a new kind of home,
With a cupcake cactus that laughs when I bite,
I've never known peace could feel this light.

I'll take my moments with chuckles and cheer,
In an open expanse where silliness steers,
As the nights roll in full of jest and of glee,
In nature's own playground, I'm ever so free.

Cradled in Warmth

The sun sets slowly, a golden embrace,
While sand hugs my toe, what a funny place!
My shadow does dances like it's on stage,
And giggles escape, it's all the rage.

Warmth wraps around like a cozy old quilt,
A treasure of joy, yet somehow I'm spilt,
I tumble like tumbleweed, rolling away,
Chasing after laughter at the end of the day.

Stars come to play in their twinkly garb,
While I swap my tales, oh boy, it's a barb,
With giggles that echo across the night sky,
Finding humor as sweet as a berry pie.

Cradled in warmth where worries do cease,
Even the coyotes join in on the peace,
With chuckles and chuckles, the night wraps me tight,
In this humorous haven, everything's bright.

Tapestry of Time

In a world where seconds flee,
My watch ticks like a bumblebee.
Each moment a mosaic bright,
Woven patterns in the light.

When hours play a game of hide,
I chase them, but they swiftly glide.
Time giggles, hiding behind a cloud,
As I dance, a bit too loud.

With every tick, I shout, 'Oh dear!',
While minutes wink and disappear.
But laughter lifts the weight we bear,
A tapestry in carefree air.

So here I am, a jester bold,
With golden threads of tales retold.
In life's grand clock, I'm just a mime,
Jumping through the tapestry of time.

The Gentle Embrace of Dust

Dust bunnies gather, quite a flock,
They hold a meeting on my clock.
Whispers of old, they sway and spin,
In their embrace, I wear a grin.

As I sweep, they giggle and pout,
'No, please don't take our fun route!'
They hustle back to their cozy lair,
Under the couch, they play and stare.

I toss a feather, they leap with glee,
A playful dustball jubilee.
Each particle, a memory grand,
In this silly, swirling band.

So raise a toast to dusty friends,
Whose laughter never quite ends.
In their gentle, grainy sweep,
I find joy and secrets deep.

Calm in the Shifting Shadows

Shadows dance like playful sprites,
Whispering tales of silly nights.
In corners dark, they twitch and sway,
Inviting laughter into play.

I tiptoe softly, pretending to sneak,
But shadows giggle, they are not meek.
They pop out here, they pop out there,
Making me jump with silly flair.

With each flicker, they tease and taunt,
Playing tricks like a friendly haunt.
Yet in their jest, a calm I find,
A soothing balm for the busy mind.

So let the shadows leap and twirl,
With each giggle, my worries unfurl.
In this jest, I take a stand,
Finding comfort in their playful band.

Refuge Beneath the Stars

Under stars that wink and shine,
I share a snack, a drink, some wine.
The moon joins us, a friendly guest,
In this cosmic, silly nest.

Constellations giggle, so divine,
Painting stories with a twinkling line.
Yet I trip over my own two feet,
As I dance beneath their cosmic beat.

With each star, a wish I make,
But tripping triggers a silly quake.
Laughter echoes through the night,
As I fumble, oh what a sight!

So here I sit, a cosmic fool,
Beneath the stars, I find my school.
In refuge bright, the laughter flows,
With every twinkle, joy just grows.

Echoes of Lost Horizons

A snail on a quest, moves slow as a dream,
Chasing the sun, or so it would seem.
With a shell on its back and a plan of great fame,
It shouts to the world, "I'm winning this game!"

Seagulls swoop down, they want a free meal,
While the snail just laughs, 'What a strange deal!'
He slides past some clams who are busy with chat,
"Hey there, slowpoke! Want to race?" "I'll pass that!"

The horizon it beckons, all bright and so wide,
But our little friend knows he'll enjoy the ride.
With each tiny inch, his heart fills with cheer,
Trusting the journey, he's got nothing to fear.

And in the end, as he reaches his goal,
A puddle awaits, it's a shimmering bowl.
He jumps in the splash, with a spin and a twirl,
And declares, "I'm the fastest!" to the sand and the whirl!

The Silence Between

A cat on a fence, with a confident stance,
Takes a moment to ponder on life's little dance.
The dogs down below, they bark and they play,
But the cat just smirks, 'I'll nap the day away.'

The leaves whisper secrets, so soft in the breeze,
While the cat stretches long, with elegant ease.
"Why chase after mice? They're just not my speed,
I'll lounge in the sun, that's truly my creed!"

A squirrel darts by, with a nut in the air,
"Hey kitty, don't you want to come share?"
But the cat just rolls over, all cozy and bold,
"Thanks, little buddy, but I've got a strong hold."

So he sits in the calm, on his throne high and clear,
And the world goes around, while he sips his beer.
With no need for chaos, he simply will stay,
In his peaceful kingdom, where he rules the day.

Solitary Sunshine

A lone sunflower stands, in a garden so bright,
Trying hard to dance, but it's quite a lost sight.
"I'm not meant for waltzes, best stick to my roots,
Or maybe I'll jiggle—like these funny ol' boots!"

The bees buzz around, with their business to run,
But the flower just grins, enjoying the fun.
"Join me in laughter, let's toss back some shade,
While I bask in the glow of this sunflower parade!"

Yet when wind whips around and it starts to get rough,
The sunflower fumbles, "Things are getting tough!"
But then it remembers, its pollinated friends,
"All the joy in the garden, this laughter never ends!"

So it spins in the breeze, with roots deep below,
Finding rhythm in chaos, with a sunbeam's warm glow.
And who would have thought, in this patch of pure cheer,

A lonely old flower could conquer all fear?

Resting Places in the Dust

A gopher popped out, with a grin on its face,
"I've freshly dug tunnels, oh what a fine space!"
The neighbors all gathered, with stories to boast,
"Wanna see my home? I have the best toast!"

But their chatter grew loud, as they all shared their digs,
Penny the rabbit said, "Mine's cozy for pigs!"
With a hop and a skip, she invited them in,
But the gopher just giggled, "You're smelling like spinach!"

Next up was the raccoon, who claimed he had style,
"My trash can's a palace, it's worth your while!"
But the gopher just rolled, his eyes doing flips,
"I'd rather keep digging than munch on your chips."

At last, he just sighed, laying flat on the ground,
In the warm, golden dust, his contentment he found.
With a chuckle he said, "For a guy who digs deep,
Sometimes all that you need is a place just to sleep!"

Elysium Between the Dunes

On the beach, I found a shoe,
Could it be a treasure? Who knew!
With a crab, I had a chat,
He planned to start a circus act.

Seagulls swooped to steal my fries,
They screeched like they were in disguise.
I tossed some crumbs, they danced with glee,
Who knew seagulls loved gourmet free?

A flip-flop race, I joined the fun,
But the winner? A turtle on the run!
I laughed as he crossed the finish line,
I guess slow and steady wins every time.

With my sunhat blown, I ran to chase,
Balloons floating off in a silly race.
They drifted to the distant light,
And I just stood, wind-blown and bright.

Ebb and Flow of Stillness

A wave rolled in with a cheeky grin,
It splashed my toes—let the fun begin!
With every crash, it called my name,
I shrugged my shoulders, what a game!

In the tide, I lost my hat,
A seagull wore it—imagine that!
He strutted proud, a feathered king,
While I pondered what my hair would sing.

The beach ball bounced and flew away,
I chased it down, oh what a display!
Rolling past shells, I tripped and fell,
Laughed so hard, I rang my own bell.

Coffee in hand, I slipped on sand,
My drink now in my lap, unplanned!
But laughter bursts like ocean's cheer,
As I sip like a beach bum, no fear.

Horizon's Embrace

I saw a horizon dressed in gold,
Whispers of sun told tales bold.
A fish leaped high, splashed my friend,
Turns out he just wanted to blend!

With a bucket hat and beachy flair,
I built a castle—oh, with no care!
But the waves had plans, a sneaky plot,
My shore retreat? One giant splot!

I found some shells, a colorful race,
Each one a treasure, a laugh on my face.
Then a crab tried to steal my snack,
We argued till both backed off—what a quack!

Umbrellas danced in the coastal breeze,
A kite flew high, just like my tease.
Caught in laughter, I lost my sense,
But found a day that made perfect sense.

Emptiness Unraveled

An empty cooler, what a sight!
I swore it was full, now it's just light!
My friends all laughed as I sat there,
Telling tales of a beach day fair.

The sun slipped down, what a tease!
I tried to catch it—oh, if you please!
My shadow shrunk, then grew so tall,
In this wacky, wonderful beach hall.

I lost my shades, said they run free,
Two crabs in them, plotting their spree.
They strutted around, all cool and proud,
I watched, bewildered, lost in the crowd.

As the stars peeked in one by one,
I hoped they'd share a wink or a pun.
A day so silly, with little to show,
Yet in my heart, it's where laughter flows.

Beneath the Celestial Veil

Under a sky where stars do dance,
I lost my shoes while taking a chance.
The moon winked down, gave me a grin,
While I chased fireflies, hoping to win.

A comet zipped past, what a sight!
I tripped on a rock, fell flat—oh, what fright!
The constellations giggled above,
As I lay there, dreaming of love.

A raccoon joined in, stealing my snack,
In this cosmic circus, there's no looking back.
Together we laughed at the night's wild plan,
Who needs a map when you're your own fan?

So here I am, on this twinkling hill,
With a friend made of mischief and beans to spill.
We'll frolic and tumble till dawn breaks anew,
Beneath the cosmic curtain, just me and you.

Serenity in a Parched Silence

In a desert land where cacti wave,
I found a mirage that thought it was brave.
It danced in the heat, oh what a sight!
But closer I got, it just took flight.

A tumbleweed rolled with its hair in a mess,
I asked it for guidance, it said, "No stress."
With a shrug and a tumble, it wandered away,
Left me in silence, not knowing what to say.

The sun took a break, said, "Let's play hide and seek,"
I yelled, "Come out now!" but it just stayed bleak.
A lizard popped up with a fluttering tongue,
"Why not just laugh till the day is all done?"

So I laughed at the sand as it tickled my toes,
And I danced with the critters, all jiving in pose.
In this quiet expanse, I found it just right,
To find joy in the stillness, beneath the bright light.

Memories Caught in the Wind

A kite in the sky with colors so bright,
Twirled and it spun, oh what a delight!
It snagged on a branch and cried, "Oh dear me!"
But I just chuckled, "That's part of the spree!"

The breeze whispered secrets, it tickled my nose,
As I danced with the dandelions, striking a pose.
Each puff brought a story from days gone by,
With laughs and with blunders, oh me, oh my!

Caught in a whirl of laughter and cheer,
I tossed up my worries, they disappeared.
The wind wrote my name on the clouds up high,
And I tossed back a wink, just me and the sky.

So here's to the moments that float on the breeze,
To slip-ups and giggles that put me at ease.
In this playful world where memories play,
I'll hold them forever, come what may.

Whispers Beneath the Surface

In a pond where the frogs sing a tune,
I splashed with a grin, just like the moon.
The fish wore top hats as they swam by,
They threw a grand ball—I couldn't deny!

A turtle waltzed in, looking quite grand,
With a wink and a spin, took my hand.
We twirled through the lilypads, laughter in air,
While dragonflies flew with flair and a dare.

A stone skipped across, it wanted to play,
"Why sit by the shore when we can sway?"
I jumped in the water, joined the parade,
In this joyful chaos, I wasn't afraid.

So beneath the surface where whispers emerge,
I found my own rhythm and joy started to surge.
With friends in the ripples and laughter so pure,
We'll dance in the pond—there's always a cure.

Tides of Tranquility

The waves come in, they tickle my toes,
I laugh and shout as the seagull goes.
With a splash of water, my worries fade,
My sunburned nose, a badge of parade.

A crab scuttles quick, it steals my snack,
I chase it down, but it won't look back.
The ocean sings songs of joy and cheer,
While I dance like a fool without any fear.

Shells glitter bright like treasure on sand,
Fish wag their tails, they've got fun planned.
I wave to the dolphins, they giggle with grace,
As I trip on my towel, oh what a disgrace!

In the tide's embrace, the humor is clear,
Life's just a joke in the seaside theater.
With laughter and splashes, I skip, I sway,
Tides of hilarity rule the whole day!

Embrace of Desert Dreams

In the desert heat, I found my wide-brim hat,
It flew by the wind like a scared little bat.
The lizards all laugh, or so it appears,
While I tumble and roll, made of giggle and tears.

A cactus gives chase, its spikes sticking out,
But I dodge with a twist, taking the easy route.
Sipping from cacti-shaped cups full of juice,
Each sip is a gamble, but I'm feeling spruced!

Sand dunes like mountains, so easy to climb,
Except when you fall, it's a real slapstick crime.
The sun blares down while shadows conspire,
As I dance with the mirage; my feet catch on fire!

Oh, to roll in the tumbleweed's playful embrace,
Makes me forget about any desert race.
With laughter and sunburns, I claim this domain,
A laugh from the dunes, it's my happy refrain!

Shifting Patterns of Peace

Patterns shift swiftly on the vast, bright shore,
As I make a castle, it crumbles once more.
With each little wave, my plans go astray,
A sandman's too fickle to hold for one day!

The gulls squawk their jokes while circling above,
As I try to take selfies, but they mock with love.
My ice cream melts fast, it drips down my hand,
But I laugh as it races across the hot sand.

Seaglass is treasures that I've learned to find,
But also, it glimmers like my fuzzy mind.
Winds whisk my dreams like a magician's trick,
Each moment's a mix of laughter and kick.

The sun dips low, a warm golden hue,
As I chase after shadows, oh, if only you knew!
Shifting patterns of peace in this wild, fun spree,
Life's a big playground; come play along with me!

Sunlit Refuge

Under the sun, my towel's a throne,
The world is a circus, my chair's a zoo's bone.
With sunblock smeared thick on my face like a clown,
I relish the giggles while chasing the brown.

Ice cream and laughter, what more can I crave?
Except for a nap on this soft, sandy wave.
Oh, why is the sand so loyal, so sly?
As it sticks to my snacks, and I'm left to cry!

Beach volleyball games, where I'm all out of luck,
I jump for the ball but just trip on a duck.
With my best friends nearby, oh, what a relief,
Laughter erupts; it's the best kind of grief!

So here in the light, with the sea breezes blown,
In a sunlit refuge, I'm never alone.
With humor as currency, my day's truly bright,
In this playground of joy, I'll bask in delight!

Embrace of the Grain

In a world of dunes and sun,
A grain of rice was the only one.
It cracked a joke about a pot,
Said, 'I'm feeling way too hot!'

The desert lizards looked so sly,
Claiming they could dance and fly.
A tumbleweed rolled on by,
And yelled, 'Hey, I'm a fashion guy!'

Deserted Dreams

A mirage laughed with a cheeky grin,
Said, 'Wanna race? I'll let you win!'
The cactus swayed with all its might,
'I'm just here for the nightlife!'

An oasis popped up for a drink,
With coconut palms that made you think.
'Why don't we throw a wild beach bash?'
With disco balls, they'd make a splash!

Tides of Tranquility

The waves of laughter crash and play,
A seagull squawked, 'Hip-hip-hooray!'
With a shell as a microphone in hand,
  It sang the blues to the sandy band.

The sun set low, a golden pie,
'Is that a sunset or dessert on high?'
A wave rolled in, dressed in a hat,
And rolled right out with a polite spat!

The Solitude of Shifting Sand

A grain whispered tales of yore,
'The wind, my friend, it's such a bore!'
He told of camels in a race,
Who all fell down in a funny place.

The dunes would giggle, shake, and sway,
'This is the world we play all day!'
A wind-blown hat flew up and cried,
'I'm just a traveler, joy as my ride!'

Dusty Secrets

In a corner, there lies a shoe,
Lost so long, it might be blue.
A secret hiding form and shape,
Is it a boot or an odd grape?

The cat naps deep on a pile of socks,
Claiming them as her cozy docks.
When found, they shout in silent glee,
"Did you just discover a mystery?"

A fan spins slowly, dust in flight,
Making the room feel both wrong and right.
Is that a ghost, or pancake mix?
I simply can't tell—what's the fix?

So raise your glass to the dusty dome,
Where forgotten treasures find a home.
In laughter, we weave each fabled tale,
In a world where socks tend to prevail.

Unseen Currents

There's a dance in the air when you snore,
A whirlwind of sounds, who could ask for more?
The pillows revolt, taking a stand,
As dreams get confused, none understand.

The fridge hums low in twilight's glow,
While leftovers plot a cinematic show.
Pickles declare, "We want to be free!"
But mustard grins, "Not after three!"

With a generator of giggles that hum,
The walls hear whispers from chewing gum.
Balloons wear hats like they own the place,
In this wild old house, it's all a race.

So sway and jig along unseen paths,
Laugh at the world as it surely laughs.
In this playful game, mischief's our friend,
And joy's the sweet song that never will end.

Enchanted Stillness

Here lies a garden of forks and spoons,
Where they gossip of chefs and raccoons.
They've conjured a silence that begs for a chat,
About the time they baffled a cat.

An old clock ticks in a sleepy room,
Counting the seconds, chasing the gloom.
Though everyone's quiet, the cookies unite,
Rallying for laughter, ready to bite!

A turtle winks from its leafy nest,
Claiming it's part of a magic quest.
Meanwhile, dust bunnies take to the floor,
In a ballet of fibers, they're never a bore!

So gather your giggles, lend them some air,
As the enchanted stillness takes you somewhere.
In this realm of the quirky and absurd,
Every tickle of laughter is perfectly heard.

Beneath the Dusty Canopy

Beneath a canopy thick with grime,
A network of secrets and odd little rhymes.
A chair whispers tales of a bygone age,
Where it hosted dancers, all barefoot on stage.

The window's a portal to squirrels on patrol,
Chasing each other, they barter a scroll.
A slice of pizza declares, "I'm still here!"
As the ghost of old dinners doodles in cheer.

The beetle on guard does a tango quick,
With a dancer whose moves are notoriously slick.
And each fallen leaf tells a story to all,
Of laughter and ruckus in this cozy hall.

So ponder the wonders beneath this old roof,
For fun's hiding out just beyond the goof.
In everything dusty, a chuckle we find,
With joy in our hearts and laughter entwined.

Whispers in the Hourglass

In the glass, time plays a game,
Ticking softly, feeling quite lame.
Sand slips through like a sneaky cat,
Chasing after a wayward rat.

Each grain a joke that trickles by,
Winks and giggles, oh my, oh my!
A minute dances, a second prances,
Laughing at our silly glances.

Hours may stretch like a rubber band,
While I just search for where I stand.
A tickle here, a tockle there,
Time's a jester, floating in air.

So let the grains cascade and glide,
With punchlines hidden, side by side.
Let's join the laughter, not the fuss,
Embrace the silliness, just like us.

Echoes of Tranquil Shores

At the beach, the crabs decide,
To moonwalk sideways, with great pride.
Waves crash down, a foamy jest,
Seagulls jesting, they're not the best.

The sun winks down with a glimmer,
While sunscreen flies, makes people shimmer.
Buckets and spades in a wild play,
Sandcastles fall as we laugh away.

"Don't look now!" my friend yells loud,
As they trip over a laughing cloud.
The tide rolls in, a perfect prank,
Washes away the castle, oh stank!

Yet still we chuckle, hearts so bright,
Building again with all our might.
For at these shores, we find our cheer,
In every giggle, far and near.

Mirage of Serenity

A desert dream, so calm and pale,
Where mirages dance, like a fairy tale.
A sip of water, oh what a jest,
Is it real? I can only guess!

Cacti laugh with prickly glee,
As camels grumble, just let them be.
Sunbeams tease, a warmth that sings,
Whispering secrets of laughter's wings.

The dunes may shift and sway with grace,
But who can keep a serious face?
"Was that a mirage or just a joke?"
Even the cactus here just spoke!

So let's pretend, under the sun,
That this funny world is all in fun.
In every mirage, a chuckle hides,
As we traverse where humor resides.

Footprints in Forgotten Dunes

In the dunes, footprints tell a tale,
Of wayward wanderers that set sail.
They zig and zag, a silly line,
Almost as if they danced with time.

"Look here!" I shout, what's that we see?
A path of giggles, just like me!
A tumble here, a slide right there,
Every step's a reason to flare.

As we roam through the sandy maze,
Our laughter echoes in sun's warm blaze.
Each step a story, a jibe and jest,
Forging memories that feel the best.

So let's leave our footprints, wild and free,
In these forgotten dunes, just you and me.
For every stride holds joy anew,
In this sandy land, where laughs accrue.

Pathways Through the Desert's Heart

In the desert where the lizards prance,
I lost my map at the last dance.
A cactus hitchhiked on my shirt,
And laughed when I stumbled in the dirt.

With mirages teasing, my brain's a haze,
I swear they're just playing a fun little maze.
The dunes roll like waves, or so it seems,
I'm just a sandcastle, caught in dreams.

Under the sun, my skin starts to fry,
A tumbleweed passes, I think I'll cry.
Yet laughter echoes through this vast expanse,
In the desert, I'm just here for the dance!

So here's my bright plan: a picnic in sight,
With sandwiches baked in the sun's golden light.
I toast to the sun, it sips lemonade,
And the universe laughs at the jokes I've made.

Crystals of Time and Memory

In a shop filled with dust and rare old stones,
I tripped over memories, found laughs on my bones.
A crystal ball winked, said, 'Do you see?,'
'Your past is just silly - trust me, I'm free!'

My childhood snickers came whirling in,
With leaps and bounds, like a cheeky grin.
I pulled out a marble, it rolled with style,
Singing 'Don't rush, stay awhile!'

Each trinket told stories of birthday cake fights,
Of socks lost in dryers on long winter nights.
Time is a jester with a playful twist,
In this memory maze, you can't help but persist!

So I'll keep collecting the laughter I find,
Like shiny little treasures that lighten the mind.
With crystals that sparkle and giggles that shine,
Celebrating the moments, oh so divine!

Respite on the Edge of Eternity

On the brink of forever, I found a nice chair,
With clouds for my pillows, and nothing to compare.
A snack bar of stardust, oh what a delight,
I'll munch on some wishes under soft starlight.

The edge of forever has a lovely view,
Where time takes its nap, not a care in the blue.
I sipped on a comet, oh what a taste!
While a unicorn danced in a glimmering haste.

With giggles of galaxies swirling around,
I found that eternity's not so profound.
Just a carnival ride on a cosmic spree,
That goes round and round, and invites you for tea.

So here on the brink, I'll make this my stop,
With laughter and sunshine, I'll never swap.
A moment of joy, in this infinite play,
Where fun and time frolic, come out and stay!

Chasing Celestial Breezes

I chased the wind, through the stars it flew,
With giggles of galaxies, oh what a view!
Each breeze had a joke, whispered soft in the night,
'Why don't stars take vacations? Not a good sight!'

Tickling my face, the breeze started to dance,
I joined in the silliness, taking a chance.
In the company of comets, we twirled
Creating a ruckus, as the cosmos swirled.

The breeze said, 'Come, let's see what we find,
In the laughter of planets, let's bring along kind.'
So we danced through the rings of a jovial twist,
Leaving trails of fun, as if by sheer mist.

And when I returned, heart full of delight,
I swore I could hear stars giggle at night.
In chasing the breezes of laughter and cheer,
I found that with joy, there's nothing to fear!

The Wind's Gentle Lullaby

The breeze tickles my nose, oh what a delight,
As it whispers silly secrets, through day and night.
I chase its tricky path, but it just won't stay,
Like a lost shoe at a party, it's whisked away.

It dances with the leaves, a merry old tune,
Turns the mundane moments to a silly cartoon.
With each gust so cheerful, it lifts my woes,
I'm off on an adventure, wherever it blows!

Caravans of Hidden Joy

The camels wear sunglasses, what a sight to see,
They strut through the desert, sassy as can be.
With snacks packed in their humps, they travel with glee,
Singing off-key tunes of unwritten history.

Beneath the blazing sun, we all share a laugh,
Imagining each grain has its own funny path.
They roll like tumbleweed; oh, what a show,
With every wobbly step, they steal the whole show!

Lighthouses in the Wilderness

In a forest so dense, stands a lighthouse tall,
Its beams do a jig, while the crickets enthrall.
It flashes at squirrels that dance on the logs,
While raccoons in tuxedos just taunt all the dogs.

With each foghorn's honk, there's a wink and a smile,
As shadows play tag, it's a whimsical trial.
They gather for parties, though night isn't still,
A beacon for laughter, on top of the hill.

Harmony in the Whispering Wind

The wind tells tall tales of the things that it sees,
Of frogs in tuxedos sharing cups of sweet teas.
It twirls with delight, quite the socialite,
Tickling my earlobes as it dances in flight.

It brings news from the mountains, both silly and bright,
Of squirrels attending wild luncheons at night.
With breezes so charming, they serenade the trees,
And the forest falls in fits of giggling with ease.

www.ingramcontent.com/pod-product-compliance
Lightning Source LLC
Chambersburg PA
CBHW072223070526
44585CB00015B/1461